THE GIRL WHO FELL THROUGH A HOLE IN HER SWEATER

Naomi Wallace &
Bruce McLeod

BROADWAY PLAY PUBLISHING INC
New York
www.broadwayplaypublishing.com
info@broadwayplaypublishing.com

THE GIRL WHO FELL THROUGH A HOLE IN HER
    SWEATER
© Copyright 2003 Naomi Wallace & Bruce McLeod

All rights reserved. This work is fully protected under
the copyright laws of the United States of America.
No part of this publication may be photocopied,
reproduced, stored in a retrieval system, or transmitted,
in any form or by any means, electronic, mechanical,
recording, or otherwise, without the prior permission
of the publisher. Additional copies of this play are
available from the publisher.

Written permission is required for live performance of
any sort. This includes readings, cuttings, scenes, and
excerpts. For amateur and stock performances, please
contact Broadway Play Publishing Inc. For all other
rights please contact the author c/o B P P I.

Cover art by Bruce McLeod
1st printing: November 2005
I S B N: 978-0-88145-297-6
Book design: Marie Donovan
Word processing: Microsoft Word for Windows
Typographic controls: Xerox Ventura Publisher 2.0 P E
Typeface: Palatino
Copy editing: Sue Gilad
Printed on recycled acid-free paper and bound in the
    U S A

CHARACTERS & SETTING

Noil, *a young girl*
Crumbs-in-Pocket (C P), *the narrator and musician*
Lord Principal Plagueworthy (P P), *the Lord of the Castle*
Roach, Lord P P's *loyal servant*
The Mirror
The Windows & Doors *(can be played by one person or many persons)*
Itnose

Setting: at the end of the hole in Noil's *sweater*

Time: now

(Onto the bare stage stumbles NOIL *with an enormous sweater over her head. We only see half of her body as her upper half is caught and covered by the sweater. She struggles with the sweater, trying to pull it over her head. We now hear her* PARENTS' VOICES *telling her to hurry up and finish dressing or she'll be late for school. As* NOIL *struggles, she becomes very frustrated.)*

NOIL

Aaaaaaaaaarrrrrrrrgggggghhh! I can't get this horrible sweater over my head! I can't do it! I can't do it! I feel so mad! I hate getting dressed! Everyone yelling for me to hurry up, hurry up!

PARENTS' VOICES

Hurry up Noil! We're waiting for you!

NOIL

(Stands still a moment with the sweater still hiding her face) See what I mean? *(Begins struggling again)* I feel so stupid stuck in here like this. Stupid, stupid, stupid. How am I going to figure a way out? Hey? What's this? There's a hole in my sweater. A big hole in my sweater. And it's getting bigger. And bigger. *(Beat)* What's in that big hole? Oooooooops.

(Lights fade. We hear NOIL*'s voice in the dark.)*

NOIL

I'm falling. Falling. Falling.

(We hear a large thud. Then silence. Lights up on NOIL *sitting sprawled on the stage. The sweater is gone.)*

> NOIL

I fell.

(The narrator, CRUMBS-IN-POCKET, *has appeared.)*

> CRUMBS-IN-POCKET

(Sings) Once upon a time a child
while getting dressed for school
fell through a hole in a jacket

> NOIL

Not a jacket, you! It was a sweater. I fell through a
sweater.

> CRUMBS-IN-POCKET

(Sings) Once upon a time a child while getting dressed
for school fell through a hole in a sweater

> NOIL

Right.

> CRUMBS-IN-POCKET

(Sings) Well, this child was a boy child and he

> NOIL

(Interrupts) Wait a minute

> CRUMBS-IN-POCKET

(Sings) And this boy, he went

> NOIL

A girl! This child was a girl. *(Spells)* G-I-R-L.

> CRUMBS-IN-POCKET

A girl?

> NOIL

Right.

CRUMBS-IN-POCKET

Excuse me, but this is a magical adventure story and adventure stories are supposed to be about boys.

NOIL

Who says?

CRUMBS-IN-POCKET

Well, I'm not sure. *(To public)* That's what I was told by...by...by someone very important out there.

NOIL

Do you believe everything you're told?

CRUMBS-IN-POCKET

Yes...I mean no...of course not.

NOIL

Right. Let's start again. I fell through the hole, not my brother, so this story is about me.

CRUMBS-IN-POCKET

And me. So you have to guess my name. Hint: I have a cousin named bread. I was born in a pocket. I sprinkle all over the table and floor when you eat.

NOIL

Hmmm...Crumbs?

CRUMBS-IN-POCKET

That's half of my name. The rest is in my *(Nears public and pulls at his pockets)* I bet you can't guess!?

NOIL

Pockets? Crumbsinpockets. That's your name.

CRUMBS-IN-POCKET

Hello. That's me. My sister's name is
Crumbsincupboard. My brother's name
is Crumbsinbed.

NOIL

Aren't you a bit...large to be a Crumbsinpockets?

CRUMBS-IN-POCKET

I was the crumbs in the pockets of a Giant.

NOIL

Oh. Are there giants here?

CRUMBS-IN-POCKET

(Speaks with terror) Oh yes. Lots of them, and other scary
beasties and things that hiss and spew and slither and
slobber and scratch and spit.

(Begins laughing meanly. NOIL *backs away from him.)*

CRUMBS-IN-POCKET

So you better get on home, girlie. You're wasting my
time. Send your brother my way. Then I can get on with
this story.

NOIL

Look. I'm here and I'm all you've got and if you don't
want to use me in your story you can go stuff your
crumbs in whose ever pockets you choose because
I'm leaving.

CRUMBS-IN-POCKET

So what's your name?

NOIL

Lion. Spelled backwards.

CRUMBS-IN-POCKET
(*Strums and sings*) Once upon a time
there was a girl named
Lion-spelled-backwards.

NOIL
Lion spelled backwards is N.o.i.l. My name is Noil.

CRUMBS-IN-POCKET
Well, Noil, if you're going to be in this adventure you
better get started. You'll have to find your way home.

NOIL
I know. But how?

CRUMBS-IN-POCKET
Through the magic door.

NOIL
How do I find the magic door?

CRUMBS-IN-POCKET
Ah. That's the adventure. And this is going to be a very
dark, decomposing, dastardly, dimply adventure.

NOIL
And dangerous?

CRUMBS-IN-POCKET
Maybe you should quit.

NOIL
How else am I going to get home?

CRUMBS-IN-POCKET
Alright. But don't say I didn't warn you.

(*He strums wildly. Then we hear boots marching, heavily.*
NOIL *is frightened and hides.*)

NOIL

What's that sound?

CRUMBS-IN-POCKET

That sound? Scared are you?

ROACH

(We hear ROACH's voice commanding off-stage)
Tock-tick, tock-tick, tock-tick.

*(CRUMBS-IN-POCKET, suddenly scared, hides behind NOIL.
WINDOWS and DOORS enter marching and pulling a large
clock behind them.)*

NOIL

(To C P) Isn't that clock moving a bit fast?

CRUMBS-IN-POCKET

Time flies.

ROACH

(Off-stage) Tock-tick. Tock-tick. Faster! Faster! Tock-tick.

NOIL

Tock-tick?

CRUMBS-IN-POCKET

Tock-tick.

NOIL

Isn't it tick-tock?

CRUMBS-IN-POCKET

Not for these soldiers.

NOIL

Why are they marching? They don't seem very happy.

CRUMBS-IN-POCKET

Ask them?

NOIL

(Comes out of hiding) Why are you marching?

(The DOORS *and* WINDOWS *keep marching and don't hear her. She has to dodge them so they don't march over her.)*

CRUMBS-IN-POCKET

(Comes out of hiding) You see? You're not forceful enough. Where's your brother?

NOIL

(Shouts) Hey you bundle of wood and nails. Noil is talking to you.

*(*DOORS *and* WINDOWS *screech to a halt, banging and clanking into each other.)*

NOIL

That's better. Now who are you and why are you marching and pulling that clock?

DOOR ONE

We're the doors

WINDOW ONE

and windows

DOOR TWO

That must march

WINDOW TWO

as Lord P P commands.

DOOR ONE

P P stole us. Says he owns us.

WINDOW ONE

He tore us from our fixtures.

WINDOW TWO
Ripped us away from our sills, stole our views.

DOOR TWO
Broke our knockers and bells.

WINDOW TWO
We'll probably end up as firewood.

CRUMBS-IN-POCKET
Stop feeling sorry for yourselves. Noil is here to free you.

NOIL
Wait a minute. Why do I have to free them? My parents told me never to stick my nose into other people's business.

DOOR ONE
So you won't help us?

NOIL
Sorry. I have to work on getting home.

WINDOW TWO
She won't help us.

(*The* WINDOWS *and* DOORS *begin weeping and wailing,* C P *cries too.)*

DOOR ONE
(*To public)* Isn't this a sad story? Come on, cry with us. No. No. Don't laugh. Cry! Boo-hoo. Come on. Boo-hoo.

NOIL
Please. Stop crying. (*Shouts)* Stop! (*Silence)* I'm sorry you're sad. But it's not my business. Here. Let me dry your...window panes...and knobs. (*She wipes their tears.)* Please. Tell us your story.

*(*WINDOWS *and* DOORS *sing the* Song of Serving and
Obedience. C P *accompanies them with his guitar.)*

ALL WINDOWS & DOORS

March, March, March
The windows and doors march
The Big question is
Why do they march so much?

CRUMBS-IN-POCKET

(Speaks) It's really quite simple. Listen up. Hup two,
three, four.

ALL WINDOWS & DOORS

(Continue singing)
March, March, March
We must do as we're told
We must feed P P's fire,
Because he's always cold!

CRUMBS-IN-POCKET

(Speaks) How do you get people to do as they're told?
Keep them marching. Hup, two, three, four.

ALL WINDOWS & DOORS

(Continue) March, March, March
Raise the flags higher
If you don't do as you're told
You'll end up on the fire.

CRUMBS-IN-POCKET

(Sings) If you *do* what you're told, you'll end up on the
fire.

(We hear the sound of a whip. ROACH *enters, carrying a
slap-stick which he or she uses to keep the* DOORS *and*
WINDOWS *marching.)*

ROACH

Tock-tick. Tock-tick. Hey, what's going on here,
for bugs' sake? You're not allowed to stop marching.
Not ever. The clock must turn. Tock-tick, tock-tick.
That's it, you wood brains. I've got a good mind to feed
you to the termites. *(Notices public)* Ah ha. What have
we here? More troops to turn the clock? Hmmmm.
A funny set of doors and windows you are. Where's
your glass? Where are your knobs? Well, never mind,
as long as you can labor for my Lord I don't care what
you look like. Well, don't just sit there. *(Shouts)* March!
(Slaps the stick) You all now belong to Lord Principal!

NOIL

(Smacks ROACH *on the head)* Hey you, what do you think
you're doing shouting at my friends? You shouldn't
be snapping your stick at them but thanking them for
coming here to sit and watch you, you mean, horrible,
little...What are you?

ROACH

(Sings) More beautiful than a rose I am
As nimble as a bee
My voice is sweet as honey
And everyone loves me.

NOIL

Are you some kind of a beetle?

ROACH

Some kind of a beetle? How insulting! *(Sings)*
I crawl by night, I crawl by day
I never take a coach
I glisten in the moonlight
I am the majestic

CRUMBS-IN-POCKET
Roach. He's.... She's...it's a roach. If she weren't so big I'd squash her under my boot.

NOIL
Aren't you a bit large for a roach?

ROACH
I have to be big otherwise people like him would step on me.

NOIL
But why are you forcing the windows and doors to march? Can't you see they're unhappy?

ROACH
(*Circling* NOIL) My, my. You are a bold girl, aren't you? Have you ever thought of marrying an insect, settling down, raising a few bugs?

NOIL
Who do you work for?

ROACH
Ah, yes. I work for THE Lord, THE master, the Big Bug. (*Slaps her stick at the* WINDOWS *and* DOORS) You! Get in line!

NOIL
Hey! Why don't you just let them go?

ROACH
Sorry. I can't do it. If I don't do what my Lord says he'll stick a pin, a long shiny pin, right here, through my belly, and pin me to his wall with all the other bugs who rebelled. Grumbly grasshopper rebelled. Now he's in a glass box. Catarra Caterpillar rebelled and now he uses her body as a pin cushion.

NOIL

You are a coward, Roach.

ROACH

Yes. I am.

NOIL

I don't like cowards.

ROACH

No one does. I haven't a friend in the world. My own family spits on my feelers when they pass.

NOIL

It serves you right.

ROACH

But at least I have a stick! *(Cracks it)* And I can make things tock and I can make things tick. Get moving you pile of splinters!

(Herds the WINDOWS *and* DOORS*)*

ROACH

Take your complaints to my Lord. I've got work to do and time to turn.

*(*ROACH *marches* WINDOWS *and* DOORS *off the stage, slapping her stick and shouting her tock-ticks. She slaps* C P *and* NOIL *on the bottom on her way out.)*

NOIL

I should talk to this Lord. Maybe he can tell me where the magic door is.

CRUMBS-IN-POCKET

You'll have to call his magic name.

NOIL

What's his magic name?

CRUMBS-IN-POCKET

P P

NOIL

P P?

CRUMBS-IN-POCKET

Yes. Lord P P.

NOIL

(Calls) Lord P P Where are you?

CRUMBS-IN-POCKET

Not like that. Like this: Loooooorrrrrrrrrrddddddd P P,
P P, P P, P P, P P, P P, P P P!

NOIL

He's not coming. Maybe we're not loud enough.
Do you think they might help?

CRUMBS-IN-POCKET

No harm in trying.

NOIL

(To public) Listen, I need to see Lord P P because he
has got the windows and doors enslaved and I have to
tell him to set them free. Could you help me call him?
Like this: Loooooorrrrddddd P P, P P, P P, P P, P P, P P!
Ready? Loooooooorrrrrrrddddddddddd P P, P P, P P, P P,
P P, P P, P P, P P P!!

(There is a crash and thunder, lights. LORD P P *enters, in
quasi-military dress, followed by a figure dressed as* MIRROR.
The MIRROR *will stand to the side of* P P *and imitate* P P's
gestures, just as a mirror would.)

P P

What? Who? Where? *(Booming voice)* Who called me
down here? It's freezing!

NOIL & C P
(*In their fear they point to the public*) They did!

P P
You did? (*Now speaks gently to public*) Hello. Hello.
My name is Lord Principal Plagueworthy. Some people
call me Lord P P. I'm not sure if that's good or bad.
Brrrr. It's freezing here.

NOIL
Excuse me, but I need to ask you to—

P P
(*Interrupts*) Please. I don't like questions. Don't you
realize who I am? I am very important and very rich.
In short, I am... (*Takes out a sign that has V-I-R-P written
on it*) ...what you see written here.

(*He hands the sign to* NOIL.)

CRUMBS-IN-POCKET
A VIRP?

NOIL
What's a VIRP?

P P
Not a VIRP. A V-I-R-P. A Very Important Rich Person.
This is my mirror. (*He blows on the* MIRROR *and polishes it
with his sleeve.*) Whenever I forget how important I am,
which happens quite often in fact, I just look into my
mirror and see my important face and I am important
once more. My father, Lord Potty Pestilent
Plagueworthy—that's three Ps—when he died he
left me all of this. I own everything, from my castle
up there, right down to the pebbles under your feet,
including the people, their houses, their children's
potties. (*Snatches the guitar from* C P) That's mine too.
Everything in its proper place; that's two P's. Yes. I

have a big job. A really big job. Do you know why?
Because I have to spend all my time convincing people
like these that it's fair! *(Begins to cry)*

NOIL

Why are you crying?

P P

Whenever I speak about myself I'm moved to tears.

NOIL

I'm sorry.

P P

Ha! You certainly will be. You're just like the others.
That's my problem. I call it my Pesky People Problem.
That's three Ps. *(Beat)* You, Crumbsinsocks,
Crumbsinclocks, whatever your name is, hanging
about and doing nothing all day, get down on your
hands and knees and act this story out for me or I'll
feed your guitar to the fire. *(To MIRROR)* You too!

(C P *and* MIRROR *get down on all fours and act out
P P's lines, which may be miming the action of the words,
which are spoken, rather than sung.)*

P P

The people cut the wood
They sow the crops, just like they should
They harvest their labor
They hammer and glue
It's all very hard work and backbreaking too
They sweat and sweat and sweat
and I get and get and get
(P P *tears a button from* C P's *shirt.)*
Whatever they make. Hmmm. Nice button. It's not
unfair. In my very important opinion, I'm always cold
and getting colder all the time. I need tons of wood to

keep my fire burning. My fireplace is as big as a house!
Since I've chopped down all the trees in my forest

NOIL

You've started using the windows and doors as
kindling.

P P

Exactly. And now the Pesky People are complaining
that they're freezing because I've taken all their
windows and doors. *(To public)* Hey, what are you
all staring at, you preposterous pip-squeaks. I've
a mind to get you all marching. Yes, yes. Lots of
troublesome little pesky people out there. Strong
little legs! Hmmmm. Maybe...

NOIL

Look here, Lord P P, the doors and windows aren't
yours. Thief! *(She bumps him on the nose.)*

P P

Oh my. Another rebel. But, you're not a boy.

CRUMBS-IN-POCKET

That's what I said.

P P

No. You're a girl. A rebellious girl. Doubly dangerous.
Maybe even triply dangerous. *(To C P)* What's her
name?

(NOIL *shakes her head for* C P *not to tell.)*

CRUMBS-IN-POCKET

I'll tell you if I can have my guitar back.

(P P *snaps his fingers and the* MIRROR *gives the guitar back.)*

CRUMBS-IN-POCKET
Noil. Her name is Noil. *(To* NOIL*)* Sorry, but I can't sing
without my guitar.

P P
Noil. That's lion, spelled backwards. I like it. Well, Noil,
if you're a girl then you must marry.

(Suddenly drops to his knees, MIRROR *does the same,
imitating him.)*

P P
Will you, Noil, marry me, Lord Principal
Plagueworthy? You will have gold and diamonds.
You will have an enormous castle to live in, to sweep
and clean. You will have an enormous oven to cook in.

NOIL
Are you crazy?

P P
I beg your pardon?

NOIL
I wouldn't marry you if you were the last P P *on earth!*

P P
But you can't say no. I'm rich and important, etcetera,
etcetera, remember?

NOIL
I've got better things to do than wear your jewels and
sweep your kitchen.

P P
But all girls want to marry.

NOIL
Who says so?

C P & P P

Who says so? (*They each point at the other*) He did!

NOIL

Look. I fell through a hole in my sweater and I'm late
for school. I have to find the magic door so I can get
home. I'm an adventurer, not a marryer.

P P

Then I'll just have to throw you on my fire with the rest
of the rebels.

CRUMBS-IN-POCKET

Come on, Noil. All adventure stories end with the girl
getting married off.

P P

I'll let you stare into my mirror all day long....
You know. "Mirror, Mirror, on the wall, who's
the fairest" and all that sort of thing.

NOIL

No.

P P

In twenty-four tock-ticks I'll be back for your answer.
I'll marry you or use you for kindling. Either way is fine
with me. BBBBrrrrrrr. I'm freezing. Come along, mirror.
It's time for your polish.

(P P *exits. The* MIRROR *remains, weeping.*)

NOIL

Why are you crying?

MIRROR

Because I don't have a face. Everyone has a face but me.
Look. What do you see when you look at me?

NOIL

I see my face.

MIRROR

(To C P*)* What do you see when you look at me?

CRUMBS-IN-POCKET

My...handsome face.

MIRROR

(Sings The Song of the Missing Face*)*
I don't have a face, my head feels like a hole
All the faces of Lord P P have scared away my soul

In me the world's reflected
and it makes me feel dejected

Maybe it sounds silly, but I don't want to gaze through glass
Always staring at P P's face is a pain in the...
(Points to bottom, but doesn't say "ass")
How will I find a dignified place
without a recognizable face?
(To public) What do you all see when you look at me?
You see? Everyone sees their face but me when they look at me. Where is my face? I have no face. Hoo-boo. Hoo-boo.

NOIL

Excuse me. Isn't it "boo-hoo"?

MIRROR

Thank you. Boo-hoo. Boo-hoo.

P P

(Off-stage) Mirror! Hurry up. I need to look at myself.

(The MIRROR *exits, hurrying.)*

NOIL

Crumbsinpockets. I have to find my way home.
Isn't there something I can do like guess a riddle
or kill a dragon?

CRUMBS-IN-POCKET

Oh, I nearly forgot! There are three and a half things
you need to do before you can go home.

NOIL

Crumbsinpockets! What kind of a storyteller are you if
you forget the most important part?

CRUMBS-IN-POCKET

(To public) A crumby one?

NOIL

Tell me the three things.

CRUMBS-IN-POCKET

Three and a half things. Ready? Number one: You
must steal the feather from P P's hat. Number two:
Make Itnose sneeze. Number Three: Break the mirror.
Number Three and a half: Never overlook anything,
however small.

NOIL

Number three and a half? That doesn't sound right.

CRUMBS-IN-POCKET

Look. I didn't write this adventure. Just play along,
will you? Stop asking so many questions. Now, don't
forget any of the tasks or you'll be lost here forever.

NOIL

Three and a half things. *(To public)* Will you help me
remember them? *(She recites them again.)*

CRUMBS-IN-POCKET

Got it?

NOIL

Got it. Now for the feather. *(To public)* Will you help me call Lord P P again? *(Calls)* Loooooooord P P, P P, P P, P P!

(LORD P P enters, followed by ROACH.)

P P

When will the wedding take place?

NOIL

I won't give you an answer until you let me wear your hat.

P P

I can't let you wear my cap. It holds the magic feather.

NOIL

(To public) I've got to get that feather!

(As he speaks NOIL jumps up and down behind him but can't grab it as he's too tall or keeps moving.)

P P

And this magic feather is the only one left in the Kingdom. I had all the other ones burned. Do you know why? Ha! None of your business why.

NOIL

(To public) I can't get it. He's too tall. Maybe if I can get him to sit down. *(Beat)* Lord P P? I hear you can jump higher than anyone in the kingdom. But I don't believe it.

P P

You don't? Watch this. *(With great seriousness, jumps, once, in the air)*

NOIL

I've seen bugs that can jump higher than that!

P P

Roach! Hoist me!

(ROACH *stands behind* P P *and puts her hands on his waist. When he jumps, she helps lift him.* NOIL *urges* P P *to jump even higher.)*

NOIL

Higher! Higher!

(P P *finally collapses, exhausted.* NOIL *grabs the feather.)*

P P

Whew! I think I broke the P P family record for highjumping. *(To* ROACH*)* To the castle, Roach, for a nap. *(To* NOIL*)* Then I'll be back for your answer.

(ROACH *and* P P *exit while* ROACH *is speaking.)*

ROACH

You know, I really think we should watch out for her. She's a bad bug. I bet her parents were spiders.

NOIL

Well, Crumbsinpockets, I got the feather. *(She puts the feather in the pocket of her overalls, so that it is slightly visible.)* Now for the second task: Make Itnose sneeze. But who is Itnose?

(C P *shivers in fear.)*

NOIL

Who is Itnose? Why are you so scared?

CRUMBS-IN-POCKET

Everyone is scared of Itnose.

NOIL

But why?

CRUMBS-IN-POCKET

Because Itnose everything and everyone. That's why it's in exile, because Itnose.

NOIL

Because it knows what?

CRUMBS-IN-POCKET

I just told you. Itnose everything. That's why Lord P P made Itnose go far away.

NOIL

Where does Itnose live?

CRUMBS-IN-POCKET

In the horrible, dark forest. The Nosey Forest. But first you have to find the Echo Path that leads to the forest and to Itnose.

NOIL

How do I find Echo Path?

CRUMBS-IN-POCKET

You don't find it. It finds you. Just repeat after me:
Forest, Forest, dark and scary
With your boney trees so hairy
Noil must enter, like a breeze
Find Itnose and make it sneeze

(*It starts to get dark.*)

NOIL

Crumbsinpockets?

CRUMBS-IN-POCKET

Nope. This is where I exit. This is your adventure.
(He exits.)

NOIL

Crumbsinpockets! Don't leave me alone! *(Shadows of trees around her)* Don't leave me alone. *(Suddenly her words echo)* Crumbsinpockets! Come back, back, back! *(Beat)* Hey, I think I found, found, found it. But it's so dark, dark, dark. I can hardly see, see, see. *(She crawls along the path.)* How will I know, know, know, when I'm there, there, there? *(She bumps into something.)* Ouch! I bumped my nose!

(The echoes have stopped.)

ITNOSE

(We hear ITNOSE'*s voice in the dark.* ITNOSE *is very ill-tempered.)* Of course you bumped your noses. You bumped your noses on my nose.

(Lights up and ITNOSE *is visible.* ITNOSE *is a creature who is all nose.* ITNOSE *speaks with an abundance of "S" sounds in the words.)*

NOIL

Oh! My, what a big...

ITNOSE

Don't say it! Don't say it! "My, what a bigs noses you have." Can't anys of you be a little more originals? Now go aways. Who gave you permissions to enter nosey forests? Get outs! Get outs!

NOIL

Why are you so angry?!

ITNOSE

Because Lord P Ps was afraids of me and he brokes
my sneezer and now I'm defenselesses. What is a noses
without its sneezer?

NOIL

But why is Lord P P afraid of you?

ITNOSE

Because I knows all about the things he burnses
and hows he's rich because he steals from the poors.
I knows he's bads and should be eaten up by worms.
I knows and so I knows too much. If onlys my sneezer
weren't broken I'd sneezer him all overs that castle of
his.

NOIL

Well, you're in luck because I'm here to make you
sneeze. It's my second task. If I don't make you sneeze
then I won't be able to find my way home.

ITNOSE

Leave me alones. You're not smart enoughs to makes
me sneeze.

NOIL

Have you tried pepper?

ITNOSE

Of course I have, and dust and mothballs and pollen.

NOIL

Have you tried a tickle?

ITNOSE

No. I haven't tried a tickle.

NOIL

May I?

(NOIL *tickles* ITNOSE*'s nose.*)

NOIL

Tickle, tickle, tickle.

(ITNOSE *begins to respond, takes a deep breath and almost lets out a sneeze but the sneeze dies.*)

ITNOSE

Nope.

NOIL

How about this?

(NOIL *grabs* ITNOSE *by the nose and blows on it like a trumpet.* ITNOSE *begins again to sneeze but the sneeze dies again.*)

ITNOSE

See? You can'ts do it. You're just likes the others. You're not using your noses.

NOIL

Of course I use my nose. (*Sniffs*) I have a very good nose for smelling.

ITNOSE

Not that nose. Your other nose. (*To public*) Do you know where your nose is? Go on. Points to it. Not that nose you silly sneezers, but your noses. The knows here. (*Taps head*) The nose above your noses. Inside your heads.

NOIL

Look, if you're so smart, then how come you lost your sneezer? Give me that nose of yours. (*She grabs it and hangs on.*) I'll make you sneeze.

(*She spins* ITNOSE *in a circle.*)

> ITNOSE

Helps. Let go. Ah! My noses!

(NOIL quits in frustration. She sits down.)

> NOIL

I can't make Itnose sneeze. I'll never get home.

> ITNOSE

My poors, poors noses.

> NOIL

(To public) That's it! Let's use our noses, here…
(Points to head) …to figure this out. What can we
use to make Itnose sneeze? Think. Think.

*(The public should guess the use of the feather. If they don't,
NOIL can uses the feather to scratch herself or chew on until
the public "sees" the feather.)*

> NOIL

The feather? The feather!

*(She approaches ITNOSE, who is now fearful and backs away.
She runs at ITNOSE.)*

> NOIL

Charge!

*(NOIL tickles ITNOSE's nose. ITNOSE begins to gasp and
pant, preparing for a sneeze. There is a noisy and chaotic
ruckus of ITNOSE gasping and gulping air. This goes on
for some moments. And then suddenly there is a moment
of silence before ITNOSE lets loose a tremendous sneeze.
The wind from this sneeze is tremendous and loud and
throws NOIL to her knees. Now the WINDOWS and DOORS
are pushed on stage by the wind's force. They battle the wild
wind that is slowing down their march, slowing down the
clock until all the WINDOWS and DOORS collapse in a heap,
exhausted. The wind stops. The clock stops.)*

(Silence for some moments)

                              ITNOSE
(No longer speaks with extra "S" sounds. ITNOSE *is "cured".)* Has anyone got a tissue?

                              NOIL
Look! The clock has stopped. You don't have to march anymore!

                              WINDOW ONE
We don't

                              WINDOW TWO
have to

                              DOOR ONE
march anymore?

                              DOOR TWO
You mean we're

                              WINDOW TWO
Free?

                              DOOR ONE
Free?

                              WINDOW ONE
Free?

                              NOIL
Yes. The clock is broken. You're free.

                              DOOR TWO
Hip-Hip

                              WINDOW ONE
Hurrah!

ALL WINDOWS & DOORS
Hip-Hip-Hurrah!

NOIL
You better hurry on back to your villages, find the
houses you were taken from and start building again.

WINDOW ONE
Yes. Yes, there's lots

DOOR ONE
to do.

DOOR TWO
Goodbye. Goodbye.

WINDOW TWO
But first let's say—

DOOR ONE
Goodbye to this!

(They exit and we hear them breaking the clock off-stage.)

NOIL
Well, Itnose, now you have your sneezer back and I
have only one more task to do before I can go home.
Goodbye Itnose.

ITNOSE
Goodbye Noil. But remember:

(Sings The Knows Song*)*
Don't forget, Don't forget
You've got a nose, above your nose
Inside your head, The nose that knows
So let your sneezer show you...
ah, ah, ah, Choo.

Now Goodbye. My sneezer is very tired and I have to
go rest it.
(ITNOSE *exits.*)

NOIL

And I must get out of this forest.

(NOIL *crawls again. Lights dim on her as she crawls out of
the forest and exits. Lights up on* P P *at another place on the
stage. He is shivering.*)

P P

What's this terrible wind, this preposterous, punctilious
wind? That's two Ps. It's never been this cold. Time for
some more wood for my fire. Roach!

(ROACH *hurries on.*)

P P

Bring in some more windows and doors. Chop them
up. Throw them on my fire. I've never been this cold
before.

(ROACH *exits, then returns dragging the broken clock.
When* P P *sees it, he screams.*)

P P

My clock! What has happened to my ticker?

ROACH

It got tocked.

P P

Who broke it? I'll roast them alive, I'll—

ROACH

A tremendous wind, all in one blow, knocked us all
over. But I did my best, My Lord. There were hundreds
of them, swarming all over. (ROACH *begins to shadow
box.*) But I swung to the left, and I swung to the right.

P P

Quiet! You piddling, puddling, posthumous excuse
for an insect. You were supposed to protect that ticker
with your life. Now how will I know what time it is?
How will I know what time to go down to the village
to break up the houses and throw them on my fire?
(He beats his own head.) Oh my. Oh me. Oh my. Oh me.

ROACH

Excuse me, Lord P P. But isn't it: Oh me, Oh my?

P P

Not any more it isn't! How will I keep my slaves
marching in rhythm without the tock-ticks? Oh,
I am so angry I have to look into my mirror to believe
just how angry I am. Mirror!

(MIRROR enters.)

P P

Let me look at my face. *(Does so)* Yes. Still very
important. Even without my ticker. Bring in my
windows and doors. I'm going to break them board
from board, crack their panes, pull out their knobs,
bend their sills.

ROACH

They've rebelled sir. They've run off.

P P

What?

ROACH

After the ticker stopped, I couldn't keep them in line,
no rhythm for them to march to.

P P

There is only one wind that could have stopped my
clock. Itnose's wind. But that's impossible. Only my

magic feather can make Itnose sneeze and I have that
feather right here

(Feels his hat, then both P P *and the* MIRROR *scream at the
same time.)*

P P

Thief! Who stole my feather!

*(*NOIL *jumps out of hiding, with* C P *behind her.)*

NOIL

I did. And I made Itnose sneeze.

ROACH

I told you she was a bad bug.

NOIL

And now the clock is stopped and the windows and
doors have rebelled.

P P

Oh, oh, oh, oh. I am mad. I am so mad. So mad.

CRUMBS-IN-POCKET

Just how mad are you, Lord P P?

P P

I'm so mad I could...I could.... *(Looks in* MIRROR *again)*
AAAhhhh! Whose horrible furious face is that in my
mirror?

NOIL

(To public) And now I have to do task number three.

P P

Why I've never seen such a horrible face? Get out of
my mirror you horrible face! I want to look at myself,
not you!

NOIL

Let's see. I had to break something but I've forgotten
what I had to break.

CRUMBS-IN-POCKET

Better hurry up.

P P

And not only is it a horrible face, it's an ugly face,
a face that no one would listen to, a face that no one
would obey.

NOIL

I know, let's use our Knows to figure this out.
(*To public*) Was it a plate? A cup? Can you remember?

P P

(*Still shouting into* MIRROR) Get out of my face,
you ugly, mean face!

NOIL

(*"Hears" the public give her the answer*) That's it.
The Mirror! Break the mirror!

(*The* MIRROR *exits in fright.*)

NOIL

But I can't break this mirror. I was told it's bad luck
and it's none of my business. But nothing is going to
change if I don't. So I must!

(NOIL *rushes off-stage after the* MIRROR *and we hear her
break the* MIRROR.)

ROACH

Oh, oh, oh, oh, oh.

(*The* MIRROR *enters with his/her face visible, only the frame
of the* MIRROR *intact.*)

MIRROR

Hello? Hello? (MIRROR *feels its own face.*) What's this?
It's my face. I have a face! Everybody look! I have a
face. *(Runs to* NOIL*)* What do you see when you look
at me?

NOIL

I see your face.

MIRROR

(Runs to public) And what do you see when you look at
me? Oh, I'm so happy! Ee-yip! Ee-yip! Ee-yip!

ROACH

Hey, you, isn't it Yip-ee?

MIRROR

Each to one's own, I say. Finally I have my own face.
And a very good face it is.

P P

And now I have no mirror. What will I look into when I
need to remember how I'm a very important and pretty
person? That's still two Ps, isn't it? *(He weeps.)* Now I'm
a nobody. I have no order, no clock, no slaves, no
mirror.

(Collapses in a heap on the stage. DOOR *and* WINDOW *enter,
decorated with balloons and party things.)*

DOOR ONE

Well I never thought

WINDOW ONE

I'd see the day

DOOR TWO

when old Potty P P *head*

> WINDOW TWO

would break down and cry

> DOOR TWO

I suppose he's got a heart

> WINDOW ONE

after all.

> NOIL

He's crying because he can't be a mean, horrible Lord
anymore.

> CRUMBS-IN-POCKET

He's upset because now he's one of us.

> P P

That's right. Now I'm just like the rest of you. Hoo-boo.
Hoo-boo. Wait a minute. Is that true? Am I just like the
rest of you?

> NOIL

Of course you are.

> P P

Just like the Pesky People? Then it only follows that
I have the same rights as the rest of you.

> CRUMBS-IN-POCKET

Oh?

> P P

And that means I don't have to live in that freezing
castle and chatter my teeth all day and night. That
means I can live in a little house like the rest of the
Pesky People.

> DOOR ONE

Just like

DOOR TWO

The rest

WINDOW ONE

of us.

P P

But can I at least keep my name?

NOIL

That's up to the windows and doors and the mirror.

P P

Well?

(*The* WINDOWS, DOORS *and* MIRROR *huddle to discuss it.*)

WINDOW ONE

He can keep

WINDOW TWO

The Ps

DOOR TWO

But he'll have to drop

MIRROR

The Lord bit.

NOIL

Take it or leave it.

P P

Drop the Lord in front of my Ps? Then I'd only be
Principal Plagueworthy. Ugh. An ugly short name.
How about Pesky Parsimonious Portable Peter?

(*After some mumbling they all respond with variations
of "alright", "O K", "I suppose so", etc.*)

MIRROR

Then we'd better be going.

P P

Do you think I could have just a small, small mirror over my mantelpiece?

(WINDOWS, DOORS, P P, *and* MIRROR *exit, discussing the possibilities.)*

MIRROR

Actually, I have this cousin....

CRUMBS-IN-POCKET

Well, Noil. I guess the adventure is over and it's time for you to go home.

NOIL

Yes. I did the three tasks. I stole the feather, made Itnose sneeze, and I broke the mirror. Now where's the magic door?

CRUMBS-IN-POCKET

Close your eyes. *(To public)* You too. Close your eyes and repeat after me: Magical door, magical door, magical door. Poof, Poof, Poof.

NOIL

Crumbsinpockets, nothing is happening!

CRUMBS-IN-POCKET

Hmmm. *(Beat)* Poof...Poof...Poof? It always worked before.

(NOIL *and* C P *keep trying to call the door while* ROACH *speaks.)*

ROACH

Excuse me, I was wondering what's in this all for me? The windows and doors are free, Itnose found its sneezer, the mirror found her face and P P's got a new name. But what about me? What do I get?

CRUMBS-IN-POCKET
Go catch a bug. Can't you see we're busy here? Everyone close your eyes or it won't work.

(NOIL *and* C P *close their eyes and then* C P *and/or* NOIL *peek and find members of the public with their eyes open.)*

CRUMBS-IN-POCKET
Hey, she's peeking!

ROACH
But I am a bug. That's my problem.

NOIL
He's got his eyes open! Please can you close your eyes!

ROACH
No one wants to be friends with a bug.

NOIL
Stop that, Roach. If you were a little kinder and stopped ordering people around you'd find a friend.

ROACH
Would I ?

CRUMBS-IN-POCKET
Might take you a few hundred years.

ROACH
Would you be my friend, Noil?

NOIL
I can't. I don't make friends with bugs.

ROACH

Well, then I guess I'll just go away, maybe sell my body
to science. Goodbye...cruel world...

NOIL

But I might consider it.

ROACH

Would you?

NOIL

Can you play games? Build a tree house? Do a
somersault dive?

ROACH

I can learn!

NOIL

Alright. I'll be your friend.

(When NOIL *says this we see magical light and the magic
door "appears".)*

NOIL

The magic door! So that's what we forgot. The half!
The three and a half: Never overlook anything,
however small. That's you, Roach.

CRUMBS-IN-POCKET

But I wouldn't call him small. Maybe I should change
the wording to: Never overlook anything, however
buggish?

NOIL

Well, this is goodbye. I'm going home.

CRUMBS-IN-POCKET

Goodbye Noil.

ROACH

Wait! Can I come with you?

CRUMBS-IN-POCKET

Sorry, Roach. Only Noil can go through the magic door.
You belong here.

ROACH

But how will I learn to jump rope if I don't go with her?

CRUMBS-IN-POCKET

Tough crumbs, old bug. Goodbye Noil!

NOIL

Goodbye! *(She steps through the magic door and disappears.)*

ROACH

Wait!

(Blackout. We hear NOIL *struggling in the dark. Lights up
on* NOIL *struggling with her huge sweater as she was in the
beginning.)*

NOIL

What? This sweater is still stuck on my head?
Aaaarrrrrgggghhhhh!

(Fights angrily with it, then we hear her PARENTS' VOICES
telling her to hurry up.)

PARENTS' VOICES

Hurry up, Noil. You'll be late for school.

NOIL

Aaaaaaaaarrrrrrrgggghhhhh! Wait a minute. I know I can
do it. I just have to take a moment and think, use my
knows, careful, think.... They're shouting at me again,
telling me to do this, do that. Think Noil. Be calm.
I don't want to get lost again. Use your knows. There!
(Her head pops through the neck opening.)

NOIL

At last! I'm back!

PARENTS' VOICES

Hurry up, Noil. You'll be late for school!

NOIL

I'm ready! *(Beat)* Mother, Father, I fell through a hole in my sweater and I fell into a magical land.

PARENTS' VOICES

Stop daydreaming, Noil. Come here this instant.

NOIL

(To public) Daydreaming? Was it all a dream?
But what about my new friend, Roach? *(Calls softly)*
Roach? Roach? *(Silence)* Well. Who ever heard of a
girl's best friend being a roach?

PARENTS' VOICES

Noil?!

NOIL

Coming!

(NOIL *sits, remembering her friends and after some moments*
C P *appears in the "other" land.* NOIL *can see him.*)

NOIL

Crumbsinpockets!

CRUMBS-IN-POCKET

(He waves.) And so my friends, that concludes the story
of the girl who fell through a hole in her jacket.

NOIL

Sweater, you silly old Crumbsinpockets. The girl who
fell through a hole in her sweater.

CRUMBS-IN-POCKET
Oops. And so my friends that concludes the story
of the girl who fell through a hole in her sweater.
So remember:

(*All appear beside* C P.)

CRUMBS-IN-POCKET
(*Sings*) If you're always being told what to do
If you're feeling like a window or a door
If you're about to cry "boo-hoo"
Don't forget, Don't forget

ALL
You've got a knows, above your nose
Inside your head, the nose that knows
So let your sneezer show you...
Ah, ah, ah choo.

(*They are "gone". *NOIL* sits alone in her room.*)

NOIL
So let your sneezer show you. Ah, ah, ah choo.
(*She exits singing.*)

END OF PLAY

Notes for the director:

NOIL: It is important that Noil is not portrayed
as "cute", "shy", or "girl-ish". She is a smart and
courageous girl, not afraid to speak her mind;
she is never silly or frivolous.

C P: While he is the narrator, by no means should he
be played as omnipotent or overshadow NOIL in any
way. C P is a jolly, harmless musician, if not a bit of
an egotist. But, when things get scary, he is more of
a coward than the rest of the characters.

The characters of ROACH, MIRROR, ITNOSE, and
WINDOWS and DOORS can be played by either male
or female actors.

While costumes for the other characters may take many
forms, NOIL must not be dressed in any "cute" outfit,
and certainly not in a dress or skirt. She is on an
adventure, and should be dressed accordingly.

www.ingramcontent.com/pod-product-compliance
Lightning Source LLC
Chambersburg PA
CBHW061101050726
47592CB00004B/1782